Soaking In Silence

The Quest for Tranquility

Dr.Kanakamalini M.A.

BookLeaf
Publishing

India | USA | UK

Made with ❤ on the BookLeaf Publishing Platform
www.bookleafpub.in
www.bookleafpub.com

Dedication

To all those moments of silence and inner peace , the silent and soothing scenes of nature , tiny creatures that build life facing all perilous elements of nature , and all those suffering souls who never accept defeat in life.

Preface

'Soaking In Silence: The Quest for Tranquility' is a series of 21 poems describing the journey of a tormented soul from chaos to conflict. Life turns out to be a bed of thorns for some and fate seems to challenge them with its vengeful twists and turns. Gentle souls suffer from unexpected and unfair tragic events. Frustration and panic lead to hopelessness and soon the whole world appears to be against them. Perplexed and clueless, they try to seek solace but nothing works for them. Nothing pacifies them and a status of void is built. This void is filled with frustration, negative thoughts, venom and bitterness. Heart and mind become a burning furnace and get distanced from all kinds of relationship.,

"My lips spewed venom, rode on fury and let the layers of restraint to shatter."

These poems take you through the healing journey. The poems, 'My Companion' and 'Understanding Silence', signify the value of Silence. Silence soothes one's bruised heart and provides time for recovery and regeneration. There is no need to seek tranquil moments outside. They are part of one's mind and heart and one has to to discover them with patience. Silence is often mistaken as weakness and lack of agency. Silence is actually the reflection of endurance and stoicism. It reflects the inner strength one possesses. The souls in turmoil blame fate, god and the world around .They are lost in the abyss of venom and desperation. They breathe fire and writhe in self-pity. At the right time, they search for the beacon light of hope. They seek silence and silence offers its supporting hand. The process of recovery begins with earnestness. The soul's quest for tranquil moments begins in the company of silence,

"It taught me to be the earth bearing tremours, to be the banks facing floods, to be the sky holding dark clouds."

Silence takes the tormented soul on a nature's tour. It exposes the soul to the blissful moments of silence found around. In the arms of Silence, the soul prepares itself for the recovery process. The icy peaks, serene valleys, misty twilight and the calmness of the grazing herds work as soothing balm. The smell of earth wet with fresh rains, the happy shepherd going home with his flock, the aura around the lamp lit near the altar, the magical stories narrated by a grandma bring joy. The soul witnesses the silent union of long-parted lovers, the teary silence of a young father holding his newborn child and the silence of the starry nights. The silence of the inarticulate world pacifies the soul.

The journey is not just about the serene scenes. It has its sorrowful moments also.The hopelessness of the ignored mother, the deathly silence of the departed soldier's house, the unflinching silence of the fisher-woman who has nothing left to lose and the bitter silence of the toiling father mocked by his own son, display the intensity of suffering. The nature's teachers, the tiny creatures like the web-weaving spider, the ants working diligently for the rainy day, little birds guarding their nest teach great lessons of life. The tormented soul realises that life is full of perils, unknown and unexpected. Survival is the key. Life should be continued with spirit and inner strength enjoying the little joys, god blesses every being with. After watching life, in its varied hues, the suffering soul gains inner peace. There is realisation and elevation of mood and thought. The tormented soul attains tranquility and gets ready to face the challenges of life with a neutral state of mind, that is attached yet detached, like the water drops on the petals of lotus.

" Nothing is born, nothing is
destroyed, every thing originates from the cosmos,
        and merges in the expanse of the Universe."

Acknowledgements

I do thank the Book-leaf Publishing platform for providing this challenge and making me realize that I could write poetry of some worth.

Prologue

Matthew 11.28

" Come to Me, all of you who are weary and burdened,
and I will give you rest."

Bhagavad Gita 2.14 Chapter 2 Verse 14

" The wise, endowed with equanimity and intellect,
abandon attachment to the fruits of action which bind
one to the cycle of life and death, by working in such
consciousness, they attain the state beyond suffering."

1. My Companion

Poem 1

I thought of speaking to Silence,
than others, who rarely understood me
or listened to me, my speech could begin at once,
as Silence was within me, around me
and shrouded me with familiarity.
It waited for me to begin, never longed for attention,
may be it knew I would speak to it for certain.

No breaking of ice, not even a bit of shyness,
formality was marked by its absence.
No efforts were made on either side,
I just allowed it to engulf me, caress me ,1
with no din or display. It grasped my emotions in its
palm,
touched my unfathomable recesses with gentle
groping.

No shaking of hands or warm hugs, not even an

embrace,
no need of introductory smiles or initial talk.
Eyes turned inwards, just felt the touch of silent
shores,
the soothing stand-still touch of silent hands,
the soft breath of quietness, the aura of the inarticulate
world, cradled me to sleep with care.

2. Understanding Silence

Poem 2

Why I sought Silence, longed for it?
I had ignored Silence, considered it a trash,
I valued angry outbursts more, looked at Silence with
contempt.
labelled it as weakness, tagged silent suffering as
helplessness.
I mistook Silence for voicelessness, preferred to
answer,
every fiery word with more fire, every spark was
returned with a flame.

I indulged in word-war, with Silence being the mute
witness,
the verbal venom had excited me, I mocked at people
who called
Silence golden.
I ventured forward to shout, yell and even bark, the
void created

distanced me from all, I considered them wordy-feats.
I could see
words shattering homes, friendship, families, yet I
described it
as empowerment.
Silence just stood at a distance and watched me with
pity.

Silence witnessed mutely the breaking of human
bonds,
with people divorced and detached, Silence did not
intervene,
it waited silently for me to feel for
it, long for it, waiting for my raised
pulse-beats to calm down,
the burning furnace to cool and what could it tell me?
what words
unknown to me, what would the core of a being tell its
periphery?
What is that, not known to me? What can the icy
waters tell the brewing lava!

3. In Hell

Poem-3

My past-unvented sacks of pain, present hurdles, and
the imaginary obstacles I feared, all distanced me
from Silence.
I burst out, hissed like an asp, writhed like the fish out
of water,
smothered feelings erupted in jets. I could see Silence
flying away,
looking at me with fear or disgust, I am not sure, it
went farther and farther,
vanished like the mirage, I panicked at the departure
but could do nothing.

Hissing like the smoking Etna, jetting out like the hot
spring,
I spoke with intense emotions, using choicest of
words intending to hurt.
I preferred the anathema of Silence as company,
I slept in fury, ate barbed words, and carried a quiver

of
insulting words.
I framed poisonous phrases, hit back with an armoury
of words,
I erred in my choice of not choosing Silence as
company and got lost in
Hades's Hell.

I soaked myself in the sea of harshness, swam
across Pyriphelgethon,
bathed in Cocytus and drank from Acheron adding to
my woes..
My lips spewed venom, rode on fury and let the layers
of restraint to shatter
and collapse.
Alphabets danced around me showing the wildest
permutations
and combinations, framing killer words .Silence
helplessly searched for shields
but my boiling and burning heart sent it away with all
its efforts wasted.

Pyriphelgethon: The river of fire
Cocytus:The river of lamentation
Acheron:The river of sorrow

4. A Beacon Light

Poem-4

With emotions spent, passions ebbed, fire in the
heart vanquished,
body felt like the burnt coal, words drained,
composure lost,
the half-burning hearth pleaded fatigue, incapable of
anything lovable.
Choking on smoky ash, the soul searched for some
relief.
exhausted and repenting, looked around for any sign
of Silence
but Silence stood afar, still recovering from the angry
show of fire-work.

Immersed in the seething flow of dark emotions,let
down and
fallen out of grace,
prey to fury and vengeance, I could not realise where
I was!

I accepted my fate and went down unchecked and
unstopped,
only to spot the darker and deeper pits within my
proximity.
Alarmed, I looked above frantically, and could see a
dot of light
somewhere above.
I made sincere attempts to check my fall and looked
up earnestly.

I did not cry out for help as I had seen Silence as
my saviour,
I just raised my hand looking for something to cling
on,
then I could see the ascending steps. Not fearing the
abyss between,
made a desperate jump and landed on the cold, stone
steps escalating up.
the ascending steps had a lazy rhythm, but I chose
not to complain.
I just held on passing the terrifying segments of fire
and brimstone.

5. Towards Tranquility

Poem 5

The journey seemed eternal, leading me to nothing
but
the long awaited end came with someone at the end
of the
steps to receive me but the fading light deceived
my eyesight,
but I could recognise the host, felt the sense of lost
and found,
I just followed it like an obedient child, and it held my
hands firmly
assuring me of shelter. It did not utter a word , I did
not expect anything
and just moved on.

Curious like a child, I wanted to hear the voice of
Silence once,
" How it would be!" , I wondered, softer or squeaky,
rich or husky,

titillating or grave, I pleaded with Silence to open its
lips once,
for me , just for me, for me to gauge and understand.
It was stubborn,
It remained muted, not even a whisper, a fraction of a
decibel,
It remained dumb as stone.

Silence gathered me in its arms, placed a finger on
my partially
opened lips.
It did not demand any explanation, no clarification or
Justification.
It just wanted me to merge in it, I felt it said, " Be in my
arms."
I listened like a true disciple, trusted it like a child, lost
myself
and embraced it in all faith. I remembered going up
with it,
passing through the icy layers attaining tranquility.

6. In the Arms of Silence

Poem 6

Silence is an excellent teacher, it checks your desire
to hurt and
abuse,
It veils your meanest motives and darkest thoughts,
shrouds your
unripe
emotions.
Saves you the trouble of apologising and clarifying, it
keeps you unassessed
and unjudged.
It prevents you from hurried actions, aggravating
situations,
provides you ample of time to think, ponder and
weigh your words.
Silence is the interim relief amidst chaos and conflict.

Silence soaked me in its stillness, taught me the skill
of keeping quiet,

assisted me in gaining ground when the earth around
shook ,
helped me in hiding a hundred unpleasant truths, it
offered
me
the key to the safe chests within my chest to safe
guard them.
It taught me to be the earth bearing tremours, to be
the
banks
facing floods, to be the sky holding dark clouds.

Silence took me on a drive to sooth my fatigued soul,
I never knew its varied faces, the silence of the deep
forest,
the silence of the icy mountains, the quietness of the
forest ponds,
the stillness of the setting-Sun, the serenity of the
green valleys,
calmness of the lone house at the mountain top,
and the contented silence of the grazing herds.

7. Bliss of Silence

Poem 7

Silence made me watch the little bird waiting for its
mother,
little girls immersed in the act of collecting wild
berries
and flowers.
Little buds blooming into flowers overnight, plants
swinging their heads to the
rhythm of breeze.
Water droplets sleeping on the flower beds, shadows
of
forests
merging with fading light, mesmerised, I stood still,
dared not utter a word fearing breaking of that divine
silence.

I could feel the silence at the house when the baby
slept,
the silent tears welled in the eyes of long −parted

lovers,
Silence of the twilight light, silence at the prayer-hall,
and of
starry-nights,
all that was around me, but never observed.
Words seemed meaningless, heart filled, soul
satiated,
mind contented, I held on to that tranquil moment,
clinging to it
like a child.

The silent mode could capture the nobility of
forgiveness,
true love that was shy of display, the warm hug of a
friend,
love in the eyes of the little dog that followed me.
Words stood like guests at the threshold, while
silence reached the inner
chambers with ease.
Silence could read every subtle thought and feeling,
words had no task left other than leaving the scene
silently.

8. In Nature's Clasp

Poem 8

I sat silently on the stone bench watching the
shepherd driving
his flock home.
Shadows surrounding the garden, cows standing in the
corner with no
care,
little ants moving in lines like soldiers saving for rainy
day.
stars shone in infinite lines and the moon intensely
gazed at me. Birds flew home in
quiet order.
The Sun had retreated and all flowers looked alike in
the dim light,
even the wind blew in slow pace adding to the
prevailing silence.

In the dimly lit room, someone read old letters silently
,touching

every letter by heart.
An old man recalled his younger and stronger days
with a sweet smile
on his face.
The young wife waited near the window for her
partner with an eager
look.
The lamp before the altar shone with aura around it,
the cat waited
for the cooking to finish with devotion, the backyard
was engulfed
in darkness but the trees silently conversed with the
stars above.

A little bird flew across the window, two more
followed behind.
"Were they racing?" I did not know, I did not spot any
competition,
they were just playful. A spider carefully wove its web
not knowing
the future.
Weekly cleaning would wipe off its home but it would
continue
building its home, defying all attempts of destruction
displaying
silent defiance of power.

Silence can be scary sometimes as it is deep
and inscrutable.

9. Silent Union

Poem 9

They met after a long gap, the cold period was hot
with desire.
They could meet with great effort, silence and
solitude
were the two luxuries afforded, they only knew about
that moment of
freedom.
They knew not about their future, the next meeting
was also uncertain.
They just wanted to live that moment of union; they
stared at each other,
read the feelings and passions instantly, nothing else
mattered.

He looked at her glowing face, the bon-fire added to
the warmth,
she noticed his feelings for her in his eyes, he
stretched his hands

to her.
She just allowed him hers; she raised her eyes to
meet his eyes,
no need was felt for words. His eyes sang a song to
her and she listened
to it.
He could read her eyes, her eyes soaked him in
passion, she saw
lightning
and craving.
She was the pond of passion and he could dip to his
will in it.

Their eyes were immersed in each other, love flew in
between,
he could feel her anxiety, assuring was his touch.
They felt nothing around them, everything went blur,
and they were just there
for themselves,
Did he say something to her? No, he aborted his effort
knowing well
that it was awkward,
to speak or say something to spoil the gravity of that
hour,
Silence was the only medium of commune.

10. Joy of Fatherhood

Poem 10

On his hands was the little bundle, his eager hands
felt the warm
pulse.
The little one slept happily unaware of the
surrounding, the tiny fist
held his finger offering all joys of world, it felt assured
and cared.
He felt proud and elevated, the new status of
fatherhood had instantly
matured him.
The world slept in his arms and he could feel the
vibrations of joy,
passing through him, he cried silently grateful for the
blessing
received.

The rosy lips curled in content, curly hair spread on
the forehead,

little eyes closed in sweet sleep, the little being
soaked his body
in thrill.
He held it with all his softness, fearing even to
breathe, he admired its
innocence.
His heart beats merged well with the newborn, he
could see his features
on its face.
He knew it trusted him, he had assured it of safety
and security without
uttering anything, it had already filled him with joy
and pride in return.

They had signed a silent bond between them, of love
and trust.
It was instantaneous and inborn, there was no
restriction,
on giving and taking, the enigmatic contract was
signed in silence.
He thought of hundred changes to be made to secure it,
brighten
Its future,
and was ready to increase his toil, mend his ways, all
for the
new addition, for the love and light it promised, a silent
acceptance

was reached.

11. Divine Showers

Poem 11

The rain had just stopped, the wet earth smelled
sweet,
flowers still enjoyed the soothing showers, dripping rain
drops
with pleasure.
Mother nature had drenched her thirsty children, roots
lapped up water,
plants swung joyfully, little plants looked damp with
their heads bent
to the sides. Frogs were on a picnic, ants were safe
inside their cozy cracks.
The parched Earth drank water to its content.

The sky felt light relieved of its heaviness, the dark
clouds
changed their hues, the dusty roads were washed
clean,
children floated their tiny boats in great joy, little

puddles were
their seas. Farmers thanked the skies, cats were on
the warm sofas,
Old people cited the glory of rains of their
times,
grandmas told enchanting
tales of wonder and magical spirits that they knew
since their childhood days.

The serenity of the land was alluring. Changing
colours of nature were
arresting. Some pitiable souls had no eyes for the
beauty around.
They were engaged in mean acts of hurting
and insulting. The beauty that was
splashed around for every eye went unnoticed and
unseen by a few.
The lush earth and the simple joys around could not
catch their eye.
To think that I was one such soul before, made me
shameful.

12. Sorrowful Silence

Poem 12

I ventured to ask," Is Silence happiness only?"Silence responded
In its own way.
The happy pictures rolling in front of eyes vanished
like air.
Silence seemed to say, "Here is my answer."An old woman
stood near the portico
of her house looking aimlessly. She waited for none
as nobody trod the steps
of her house since a long time .The house looked
shabby without any colour.
Renunciation shrouded her silence and felt her flesh and
soul
dead.

She had nothing to say or wish, the songs in heart
were deleted

Silence prevailed in her home of fifty years,
Children had fled to far off places and she had had
almost
forgotten
their voices.
She cooked, ate and slept like a machine, there was
no taste in her food.
She was a born nurturer and care-taker, to all , all
means all,
She had no complaints, the sense of being deserted
was sedimented
in her silence.

Her inner longings, desires had dried off, she
sometimes
recalled her first son, his childhood, his pranks and
tantrums,
He had taken two decades of her life, the other two
had consumed
the rest of her life, now the last part of her life was
only for her,
The weaker, feebler part was left for her, neighbours
celebrated
festivals, marriages, deaths, in everything people
participated, but none
was around her
except silence.

13. Deathly Silence

Poem 13

Their son returned home , but in a coffin, his wide
chest bore
too many wounds, people praised his valour,
described them as
proud parents.
Thousands had gathered to salute him, but they
wanted him back,
in flesh and blood , full of life. Their only child, they
missed
his hug,
his baritone -voice, roaring laughter and energy.
His room in their
house
will be forever unoccupied and death like silence will
prevail
there.

He will smile only in his photos; their house will be a

grave,
His special food will never be cooked, his bike will
remain covered
and dust-filled in a corner, his medals will be on the
wall, telling
stories of valour. Tears drained, emotions scorched,
the old souls
search for solace in each other's eyes, but they spot
more pain and
depression. They seek solace in silence , words can
never
voice their pain.

The mornings will remind them of his walks and cycle
rides,
afternoons flay them with loneliness and emptiness.
Evening times moist their eyes with the memory of
the son-set
nights make them fondly recall his long phone calls,
caring tone
assurance of being with them always, young men of
his age bring in them
the desire to hug him and hold his firm hands, they
find themselves in
the silent hell.

14. A Missed Step

Poem 14

She had knitted cute looking sweaters for it, planned
wall colours,
a mixture of pink and blue, had planned its arrival,
chosen baby names.
A cradle with a parrot hanging above was selected
with care,
Thought of giving a break to her career for the new
arrival,They were ready for their first child, often
enjoyed the
kicks
of the little one with thrill, and waited for the date in
great expectation.

She had changed her choice of food, changes in her
slim body were
accepted, they took delight in their transformation,
from care-free couple
to caring parents, he drove his bike slowly, she kept

all her body-hugging
dresses safely locked in her wardrobe, walked down
the steps carefully.
Listened to her mother with eager eyes, took all
lessons on motherhood
avidly, she had just changed in every way.

The glow in her eyes matched the Sun-rise; her slow
gait had grace,
Her eyes dreamt of the new-born, her face glowed
with joy,
She took easy measures of steps in the garden,
listened to sweet music,
watched funny movies with laughter and life,
browsed for little dresses,
ate to her content, never went near her favourite
street food, but
a simple fall, a missed step, put an agonising end to
all and silence
came to stay with them.

15. Silence of the Seas

Poem-15

I could see the lone woman on the sea shore
watching the
thunder storm calmly,
a fisher woman, can we call her Marina ? Names do
not matter
anyway,
She waited for none; the sea had swallowed her son
on one
such stormy day,
He was not lost in sea, his dead body was borne
home, she had no
anxieties to suffer, Storms no more threatened
her, she was spared of
hours of anxiety fearing the worse.

She looked peaceful, free of trauma, sure of her fate,
nothing more to lose now, nothing to gain, life for her
was on the neutral gear, her silence matched the

roaring sea,
She looked at the tides with no emotions, they did
not mean
anything to her , sometimes the sea appeared to be
calm,
may be it tried to match her silence but could not.

Years ago, huge waves had taken away her dwelling,
they called the tides Tsunami. She had spent days in
the church,
accepted distributed- food, clothes, mattress,
bed-sheets, all
donated by others. She had never taken anything
free from any one,
even on fish-less days. Tsunami had turned her into a
beggar,.
She was the first to return to her lost village, to rebuild
it
in sad silence.

16. Bitter Barbs

Poem 16

"You are a failure", the son said, "You want me to
cycle my way
to college, just like you did your whole life, you are
stagnant water,
with no progress, no quality, you want me to rot in this
hovel."
Father had no shield to hold those bitter barbs, he
chose
Silence to shield him. He just looked at him .He
seemed to say,
"He knows not what he is saying." Silence was the
only response he showed

Silence strengthened him to continue his toil, He had
worked hard,
to free his family from the cesspool of poverty. He
could not do much
but to be called a failure, stagnant water was more

than he could bear.
After his fuming son left he wiped his silent tears .
He could not get the boy
the bike of his dreams. He had cycled all his life, and
he had opted to buy
one for his son. The boy could not take it, but calling
him a failure!

Father remembered his own father, who was never a
father to him,
His drunken dances, wife-beating sessions had
bittered him,
In his heart he wished him dead, but never said it to
his face.
He was a pest to the family, his foul tongue, lusty acts
at night had
distanced him, but he never called him a failure. He
had sold him
to the garage people for a few thousands, but he
never called him a failure.

17. Life in Varied Hues

Poem 17

I could feel the silence after the quake, the agonising
scenes of
towns and villages in ruins, Silence on seeing years of
toil in dust,
Silence on losing all your stakes in the battle, the
silence after the war,
helplessly watching your dear one struggling for
little air
the shocking silence after an unexpected betrayal
and back-stabbing,
Silence on seeing your dream home in ashes.

Silence of loneliness during times of infirmity,
Silence of poverty in bearing insults and contempt,
Silence of
extreme hunger,
Silence on being refugees in your own country,
silence on forced

migration, Silence of the mother sparrow on finding
her nest empty,
Silence of a climber on finding an icy grave holding a
fellow-climber,
Silence of a doctor when the newborn does not
respond.

Silence in the eyes of orphan children, silence in the
eyes of
a defeated person,
Silence in the house with empty vessels, silence of a
patient on finding
death imminent.
Silence in the eyes of a deserted pup, the pain of a pet
dog cruelly
left on the streets,
Silence of a young girl molested, groped by lusty
hands inappropriately,
Silence of a father on finding his son going astray, not
being a
supporting pillar but a burden of wasted dreams and
ruined hope.

t

18. Facing the Truth

Poem 18

The sad pictures of silence made me wiser, I kept
calm,
I am not the lone sufferer, sufferings do vary in their
intensity and depth. Patience and silence become the
armours
of the sufferers, wise and calm people challenge the
vagaries of fate,
they crumble not under the wheels of fortune, never
collapse,
they just bear the burden with nerve and strength

No storm can break their calm, they disappoint fate
by accepting the challenge. They neither blame God,
nor their
Ill-luck,
They do not turn their faces away from the hardships,
they
challenge the tragic patterns of life by facing them

with inner
strength.
Why is life cruelest to a few? No one can answer this
painful
question.
some call it *karma*, some bad luck, some others call it
vagaries
of nature.

I shed tears of understanding, marveled at the silent
sufferers,
admired the strength of people who stood like rock
amidst chaos,
cried with unhappy mothers, learned to swallow hot
cinders in silence.
Empathised with the parting lovers, felt the shock of
losing one's little eggs
felt the bitterness of the helpless father, shivered with
the loneliness of the
the ignored mother, felt hurt by the sadness of the
little dog, I understood
life and its vagaries well.

19. Survival is the Key

Poem 19

The varied pictures of silence, some touchingly sad, some
vividly joyous, soothed my mind. Wiser and mature,
ripe and understanding,
I could look hardships straight in the eye.I could bear
betrayal and backbiting
stoically, could guard myself from verbal warfare,
stand firm and rooted
like a tree, unperturbed like stone. I thought of
solutions than problems.
I drew strength from simple souls who fought life's
battles unflinchingly.

Like Bruce from the spider, perseverant and patient,
I learned to weave the web of life calmly. Ants proved
to be the best
teachers, doggedly saving for the rainy day .Little
birds , steadfast and pertinent,

taught me the art of building life amidst threats and
perils.
little bees showed me the way to be stinging at times
but storing only sweetness.
I was little ashamed of ignoring these natural
teachers around me.

World is full of threats and perils but also abounds
in sweetness.
happily grazing deer have their moments of fear,
freely flying birds
do face threats from bigger birds of prey. Happily
hopping, friendly frog
ends up in snake's colon, thirsty wild cows are
dragged away by the crocs,
inquisitive rabbits are torn apart by foxes , the
tough looking male zebra is hunted
by hungry pride of lions, life is all about survival
amidst conflicts.

20. The Mystical Ascent

Poem 20

Silence seemed to have read my thoughts. It seemed
to say,
"You have seen my two faces, want to see the other
one?"
perplexed I raised my eyes in confusion, " the other
one!"
What could it be like? Silence let me peep through its
mystic layers.
I was made to go up keeping my steps carefully
through the foggy way.
I struggled to find my way up but something in me
kept me going.

The winding, ascending staircase was challenging,
but the light at the top
allured me .It was an awesome climb up. I felt
elevated. I felt attached ,
yet detached,

I was happy, yet not happy. I was there but not there,
I felt like a little
speck of light
moving towards the Sun.I kept moving on but found
myself at the same place,
felt light as feather
but not outside gravity.
I was flying in air but rooted in Earth, I felt free,
unaffected,
untouched by everything around, I was smaller than
the atom but bigger than the
Universe.

I could go up as far as I can, my ascent was rhythmic
as if pulled by some unknown force, bright, mighty
and enigmatic.
Where is it taking me? I wondered for a moment but
stopped thinking
about it.
My aim was neither going up nor going down. I was
just drawn up
by that force.
I passed icy peaks, silver like clouds, pristine lakes,
grazing unicorns,
moons and planets moving around me like burning
balls.

21. Wisdom

Poem 21

I realised, every being is there as it is destined to be
there,
nothing can be emanated or consumed. No one can
destroy you unless
you wish to be.
Nothing is born, nothing is
destroyed, everything originates from the cosmos,
and merges in the expanse of universe. Nothing
remains behind, neither
name, nor fame or feat. Every achievement thought to
be ever present
sublimates into nothing like an air bubble.

I kept climbing aiming to reach the aura of light,
passed through bright layers of light of varied hues,
powerful and almost blinding, some milder areas of
light with
soothing lights, some layers with infinite specks of

light twirling

in all patterns, some darker areas suddenly expanding

into incessant

beams of light .The play of light, bright, mild, dim,

flickering, and eye blinding,

slightly drew me into a state of stupor.

I remained in that state for hours, or days, it was a

timeless

feeling, having been lost in that aura of light. I gained

my understanding

after hours of that divine merge and got up in my

original state,

on earth, in flesh and blood, being human. With tears

in my eyes

I moved towards my life to manage my worldly

duties,

and of course , like the water drops on petals of lotus.